Get AHEAD in COMPUTING

Awesome ALGORITHMS and Creative CODING

Clive Gifford

WAYLAND

First published in 2015 by Wayland
Copyright © Wayland 2015

Wayland
338 Euston Road
London NW1 3BH

Wayland Australia
Level 17/207 Kent Street
Sydney, NSW 2000

Commissioning Editor: Debbie Foy
Project Editor: Caroline West (Blue Dragonfly Ltd.)
Designer: Mark Latter (Blue Dragonfly Ltd.)

A catalogue record for this title is available
from the British Library.

ISBN: 978 0 7502 9216 0
eBook ISBN: 978 0 7502 9217 7
Dewey number: 005.1-dc23

Printed in China

Wayland, part of Hachette Children's Group
and published by Hodder and Stoughton Limited

www.hachette.co.uk

Disclaimer: The website addresses (URLs) included in this book were valid at the
time of going to press. However, because of the nature of the Internet, it is possible
that some addresses may have changed, or sites may have changed or closed down
since publication. While the author and publisher regret any inconvenience this may
cause the readers, no responsibility for any such changes can be accepted by either
the author or the publisher.

Note to reader: Words highlighted in bold appear in the Glossary on page 30.
Answers to activities are on page 31.

Contents

Coding your World

HELP!

Computers are everywhere. Whenever you heat food in a microwave, watch an animated movie or play with a smartphone, you are using computer technology. But all this technology won't work unless you tell it what to do.

Helping hands

Although computers may seem very powerful, they need people to lend a hand. Computers can't act on their own and always need a series of instructions to tell them what to do. These instructions are called programs. Writing programs is called **coding** and is carried out by people known as coders, or **programmers**.

With a program installed, computers' big brains can run super-smart code to do amazing things. For example, in 1997, IBM's Deep Blue computer running a chess-playing program beat the World Champion chess player, Garry Kasparov. Result!

IT'S YOUR TURN

1 0 1 1 0 1

I think there is a world market for maybe five computers.

IBM 1410 computer in use at the Ford Motor Company in 1969.

TRUE STORY

Computers Galore Thomas Watson, who was once chairman of IBM, made this prediction in 1943 when computers were first invented. How wrong he was! There are now over 2,000 million computers in the world and millions more **smartphones** and tablets.

COMPUTER Hero!

The world's first computer programmer was a Victorian woman called Ada, Countess of Lovelace. Her friend Charles Babbage tried to build the first computers. In 1842, Ada wrote a series of instructions to do some complicated maths on Babbage's machines if they were completed. Ada had written the first computer program!

Ada, Countess of Lovelace

Algorithms in Action

All computer programs rely on algorithms. These are sets of step-by-step instructions to perform tasks or solve problems. Coders use algorithms to help them plan out their programs.

Everyday algorithms

You use **algorithms** all the time, probably without even knowing it. Recipes for making different foods and drinks are types of algorithm. For example, when you make a glass of squash, you know to open the squash bottle, pour the squash into a glass and then add water. The algorithm for this task might be written as:

 1. Remove squash bottle top

 2. Pour squash into glass

 3. Turn on tap

 4. Fill glass up with water

 5. When glass full, turn off tap

6. Drink!

Share the sweets!

You also use algorithms to solve problems. Say you've been given a big bag of sweets, but have to share them equally. You need to find a way to share the sweets out. Here are two algorithms for doing this:

Sweet Sharing: Algorithm 1

1. Arrange everyone in a circle
2. Hand out one sweet to each person in turn
3. When everyone has a sweet, give yourself one
4. Repeat steps 2–3 until all the sweets are gone

Sweet Sharing: Algorithm 2

1. Count all the sweets
2. Count how many people there are
3. Divide number of sweets by number of people
4. Give each person the same number of sweets as the answer

Different methods, same target

Just like the sweet-sharing algorithms, there are many computer algorithms that can do the same job. Programmers spend lots of time thinking through their algorithms, trying to come up with the fastest or most efficient way to perform a task.

Here are two different algorithms to tell a robot how to build a brick wall. Which algorithm do you think will get the wall built most quickly?

Robot Bricklayer: Algorithm 1
1. Go to bricks and pick one up
2. Return to wall
3. Place brick on wall
4. Repeat steps 1–3 until no bricks left

Robot Bricklayer: Algorithm 2
1. Go to wheelbarrow and push to bricks
2. Fill wheelbarrow with all the bricks
3. Push wheelbarrow to wall
4. Place brick on wall
5. Repeat step 4 until no bricks left

STRETCH YOURSELF

Write Instructions for a Recipe
Can you and a friend each write an algorithm for making a meal that you both like? Use lots of steps to make the recipe really clear. Compare your results:

☞ Did your friend come up with something that you didn't think of?

☞ Can you think of another recipe method that would give you the same result?

My Recipes

Ones and Zeros

All computers are packed with electrical circuits. These carry tiny pulses of electricity that act like a code, sending data as streams of just two numbers – 1 and 0.

 Number systems

You use the **decimal,** or base 10, number system every day when you are counting or doing sums. The decimal system contains 10 different digits (0, 1, 2, 3, 4, 5, 6, 7, 8 and 9). When you want to count higher, you add an extra column on the left and continue counting – 10, 11, 12.

Binary is another number system. It uses only two numbers – 1 and 0. When you want to go higher than 1 in a column, you put a 1 in the next column on the left and then start counting from 0 again in the first column on the right. Below is a table showing the binary numbers up to 15.

DECIMAL	0	1	2	3	4	5	6	7	8	9	10	11	12	13	14	15
BINARY	0	1	10	11	100	101	110	111	1000	1001	1010	1011	1100	1101	1110	1111

STRETCH YOURSELF

Change Decimal to Binary

Look at the method on page 9, then see if you can work out what these three decimal numbers (right) are in binary?

Draw five columns on a piece of paper to help you. Which numbers do you need to make the decimal number? We've done number 15 as an example.

16
17
21

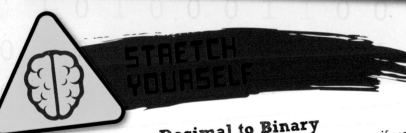

16	8	4	2	1	= 15
	1	1	1	1	

So, binary number 1111 is decimal number 15.

Remember you can use each number only once!

Answers on page 31

Column calculations

Binary can be turned into decimal numbers, and vice versa. You just need to remember that each column of a binary number is worth twice as much as the previous column. So, the first five columns of binary numbers equal 1, 2, 4, 8 and 16 if they are written as decimal numbers. The first column is always on the right, and you add new ones on the left.

If you write a binary number underneath the columns of decimal values, you can work out the value of the binary number. All you need to do is add together the decimal numbers that have a 1 beneath them.

Convert binary number **101** to a decimal number:

Columns

Decimal   16   8   ④   2   ①
Binary   1   0   1

= ④ + ① = 5

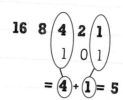

HELPFUL TIP: The binary numbers show which decimal values to add together!

Add together the decimal numbers that have a 1 beneath them.

So, binary number **1 0 1** equals decimal number 5

Convert binary number **10010** to a decimal number:

Columns

Decimal   ⑯   8   4   ②   1
Binary   1   0   0   1   0

= ⑯ + ② = 18

Add together the decimal numbers that have a 1 beneath them.

So, binary number **1 0 0 1 0** equals decimal number 18

STRETCH YOURSELF

Become a Binary Spy!

Make a secret number system on your left hand by using washable ink to write 1 on your little finger, 2, 4 and 8 on your other fingers and, finally, 16 on your thumb.

You now have a binary code machine. Any finger (or thumb) sticking up equals a binary 1. Can you tell a friend (without speaking) what number you are thinking of just by using your hand?

Here are some examples:

 Close your fist up = 0

 Give just a thumbs-up = 16

Stick up your three middle fingers = 14 (8+4+2)

Now it's your turn… Which fingers do you need to hold up to make 6, 10, 13 and 20?

Mind your Language

Early computers were programmed using long series of binary numbers. These took ages to key in and also to check if a mistake was made! The invention of the compiler allowed programming languages to be created, which made coding easier.

Computer talk

A programming language is made up of commands or instructions that are like building blocks. Coders arrange these blocks in different ways to build code and programs. The language takes care of tiny but important details such as how to add up two numbers or where to store data. Some well-known computer languages are described here.

BASIC

Your parents probably used this when computers first entered homes in the 1970s and 1980s. BASIC used English language commands, with each command placed on a numbered line. For example, the program below will display rows of 'Hello Mum' messages on a computer screen:

```
Hello  Mum
Hello  Mum
Hello  Mum
Hello  Mum
```

 10 Print 'Hello Mum'
Print means display on the computer's screen.

 20 GOTO 10
GOTO is a BASIC command to jump to a different line number.

10

JAVA

This is used to write small games and programs for smartphones, tablets and computers. Java is also used for making animated cartoons on web pages.

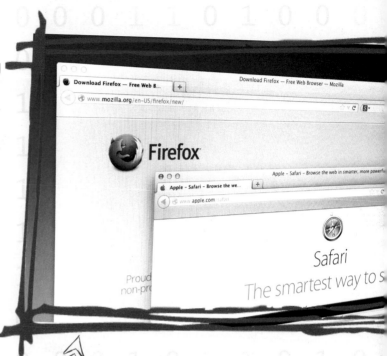

SQL

This language was developed by IBM and is used to create **databases**. A database is an application that stores large amounts of information in an organised way, so that you can find it again easily.

C++

This advanced and very powerful language has been used to write many famous computer programs. These include Microsoft Office and **browser** programs such as Google Chrome and Apple Safari that are used for viewing web pages.

COMPUTER Hero!

In 1952, **Grace Hopper** built the first **compiler** program called the A-0 system. Grace believed that computers should be programmed using commands written in English and worked hard to make programming languages that could do this.

11

Languages for Learning

Every programming language has its own commands and ways of doing things. Some languages aren't that diffcult and are designed for people to learn coding... including you!

STRETCH YOURSELF

Answers on page 31

Speaking LOGO!

The LOGO language was invented by an American scientist called Seymour Papert in 1967. It let children program a little robot called a turtle to move around the floor. Typing a command such as Forward 20 steps would make the robot move forward 20 steps, whilst typing Left 180 degrees would make it turn round 180 degrees (half a circle). Some turtle robots carried a pen so you could program them to draw on paper.

Control the Turtle

The LOGO language uses simple commands to make the turtle draw different shapes. Try using LOGO to work out the answers to these questions:

☞ Which one of the following shapes would this LOGO program draw?

Forward 100 steps
Left 120 degrees
Forward 100 steps
Left 120 degrees
Forward 100 steps

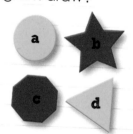

☞ This LOGO program makes the turtle draw a rectangle. Can you alter the first and fifth lines to make it draw a square instead?

Forward 120 steps
Right 90 degrees
Forward 100 steps
Right 90 degrees
Forward 120 steps
Right 90 degrees
Forward 100 steps

Infant K–1 Roamer

Other programming languages include Kodu, Python and Scratch (see pages 14–15). Kodu uses pictures as programming commands to make fun cartoons and simple games on some personal computers and the Xbox 360 games console. Python is a text-based programming language that uses familiar-sounding words. Although Python can take longer to learn, you can use it to write many types of program.

The robots are coming!

Many schools have mobile robots such as Roamers or Bee-Bots that you can program to move. You press buttons on top of the robot to enter a series of commands. These commands form a simple program. When you press 'Run' or 'Go', the robot carries out the commands you entered in their exact order.

You can program this fun Lego Mindstorms robot to move around.

STRETCH YOURSELF

Robot Rocket Launch Challenge

This set of commands describes the first eight movements the robot has to make to follow a path to his rocket. Can you work out the remaining nine commands he must follow to reach his rocket?

1. Move forward 1 space
2. Turn to the right
3. Move forward 1 space
4. Turn to the left

5. Move forward 1 space
6. Turn to the left
7. Move forward 2 spaces
8. Turn to the left

Answers on page 31

Scratch!

Scratch is one of the most popular learning languages used in schools. Scratch lets you mix sounds and pictures to create fun games and animated cartoons.

Sprite right

Scratch programs are called scripts. They feature pictures of little characters called sprites. You can program a sprite to move, change appearance, say little messages in speech bubbles or do something when they touch things or come across other sprites.

The first sprite you'll see in this language is a cat called Scratch. Other sprites include dinosaurs, bears and ghosts, or you can draw your own.

Stage

Palette

Scripts area

Scratch the Cat

Scratch screen

A Scratch screen has three main parts: the palette, scripts area and stage. The palette stores all the Scratch instructions (called blocks) that you can use. You can pick and move the blocks from the palette to the scripts area, where you snap the blocks together to build a script to create your program. Your Scratch program is then displayed on the stage.

Many types of block are used in Scratch. These are all colour-coded. You snap together the different blocks to build a program. Below are the ones you'll probably use the most:

MOVE 10 **STEPS**

Motion
Blocks like these make the sprites move across the stage and change direction.

PLAY **SOUND** MEOW ▼

Sounds
These blocks play sounds. You can pick a sound, such as a drum or cat's meow, or record and add your own.

WAIT 3 **SECS**

Events
These blocks control when parts of the script run, such as repeating some of the script or waiting a few seconds first.

SAY HELLO **FOR** 2 **SECS**

Looks
These blocks show different things such as a speech bubble or a change of costume for your sprite on the screen.

STRETCH YOURSELF

Explore Scratch!
Look at this Scratch program of a DJ cat mixing sounds. You can add to these sounds by pressing some of the keys on your keyboard. Just type this address into a web browser:

 http://tinyurl.com/watchdjcat

Check out other people's Scratch programs by typing this address into a web browser:

 http://tinyurl.com/starter-projects

Click on each screen to load the program and then on the green flag to start. You can find out what blocks were used to make each program by clicking on See Inside.

Accurate Algorithms

Computers need more precise instructions than you. A computer will only do what it is told and so needs to be instructed very carefully. This can take lots and lots of steps.

Be precise

People have to be very accurate when creating algorithms. Missing out important steps or getting one wrong can mean the program doesn't work. For example, an algorithm for a robot to walk forwards needs to contain steps that tell the robot to stop if it reaches a cliff edge. Otherwise, it will continue walking and fall off!

Here is another example of an algorithm, this time for brushing your teeth:

1. Turn on tap
2. Squeeze toothpaste tube
3. Use brush to clean teeth
4. Put cap on toothpaste

The algorithm doesn't say what sort of brush to use, to take the cap off the tube before squeezing it, or to turn off the tap. Oops! What steps could you add to make this algorithm work better?

TRUE STORY

$1 Million Lost In 2010, a new computer program to buy oil for an American company was switched on. But the algorithm had no limit on how many orders it could make — and so it made thousands. Experts think the company lost over $1 million in less than five seconds!

A-Maze-ing Algorithms

Build a maze with boxes and cushions. Write an algorithm of the step-by-step movements you would have to make to travel through the maze without bumping into any of the obstacles.

Blindfold a friend or parent and read out the commands in order and one at a time. They have to do exactly what you command.

Now, ask yourself these questions:

☞ Did your algorithm work first time or did you have to make any changes?

☞ Do you need to add extra steps and commands to your algorithm?

☞ How many runs of your algorithm did you need before it worked perfectly?

An answer for everything

Coders have to think through every possibility in their algorithm. This includes what they would like to happen, but also all the things that could happen. For example, a quiz game algorithm may only need 'yes' or 'no' answers. But if the user types in a different word, the algorithm would have to say that it only accepts 'yes' or 'no' answers and ask the question again.

Breaking things down

Many tasks are made up of much smaller ones. A good algorithm breaks a task down into as small a series of steps as possible. This is called decomposing. For example, you could break down an algorithm for making breakfast into smaller tasks such as make toast, pour glass of juice and boil egg. Each of these can be broken down into smaller steps.

Get in Step

The steps in an algorithm have to be not only precise, but also in the right order. If you get the steps in the wrong order, then the algorithm is unlikely to work properly.

Jumping around

Keeping track of the steps in an algorithm can become more complicated if it is designed to jump back to an earlier point. This simple algorithm (right) keeps track of a footballer taking shots at a goal. But the score isn't going up each time he scores. Can you work out what is wrong with the algorithm?

1. Score = 0
2. Player shoots
3. Was a goal scored?
4. If a goal wasn't scored, go to line 2
5. If a goal was scored, add one to Score and go to line 1

This algorithm almost works, but every time line 5 adds one to the score, it jumps back to line 1, which sets the score to zero again! The solution is simple: line 5 should end with 'go to line 2'.

STRETCH YOURSELF

Can You Fix the Instructions?
Here are some instructions for having a bath, but they're all jumbled up. Can you put them in the right order?

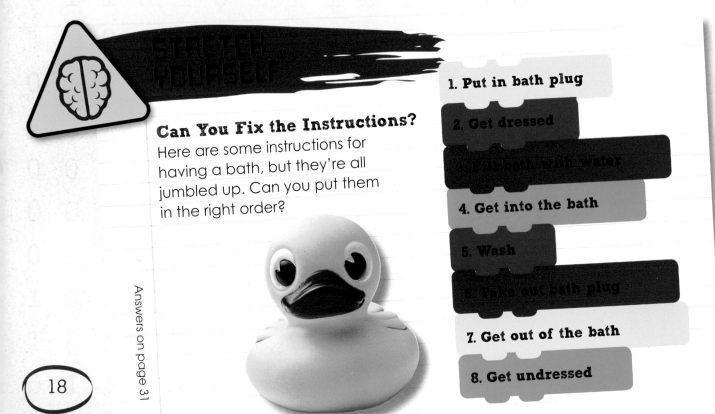

1. Put in bath plug
2. Get dressed
3. Fill bath with water
4. Get into the bath
5. Wash
6. Take out bath plug
7. Get out of the bath
8. Get undressed

Answers on page 31

18

Make Lightbot Move!

If you have Internet access, why not visit and play with Lightbot? This fun game lets you choose from a series of simple commands to build a program that will make the little robot move.

The tasks start off easy but get harder, so you really have to think through what commands to use and in what order.

You can visit Lightbot by typing this address into a web browser: http://tinyurl.com/light-robot-game

Subroutines

Some parts of an algorithm, such as displaying a message on screen, may be needed again and again. But this means that the algorithm can get very long. So, clever coders write these parts as sections called **subroutines.**

Coders only have to write a subroutine once and then direct the program to jump to it when it needs to use it. This makes writing complicated programs easier and faster.

HIGH SCORE
768.987.000

In this game, when a player shoots a spider, the program goes to a subroutine to show an explosion and then another subroutine to add points to the score displayed on screen.

Decisions, Decisions

Most computer programs have to make decisions along the way. Although some decisions are simple, more complicated ones need to be broken down into lots of small decisions.

If... Then

Many programs ask a computer to make decisions based on the information that they receive using an IF statement. This states that IF something is true, THEN the program will respond and do something.

In computer programs, decisions are made all the time. For example, in the car-racing game below, the game's code has to make lots of different decisions. Then, when the program for the race decides that the game should end, it runs a particular piece of code to give the player a final score and prints 'Game Over' on the computer screen. This is called **code selection**.

If the player presses the accelerator, **then** speed the car up

If the car bumps into another car, **then** slow the car down and make crashing sound

If the car runs out of fuel, **then** game over

If the player presses the brakes, **then** slow the car down

If the player's car is in first place, **then** display message 'You're in the lead!'

Some decisions are made in programs using different symbols to compare data. These include the greater than **>** and lesser than **<** symbols, which are used to compare numbers. For example, a program to grade the results out of 10 in a child's spelling test might look like this:

Lists of objects or numbers can be sorted out by making decisions. For example, a program might compare different numbers to work out which are bigger and which are smaller.

A series of decisions can be shown in a branching tree diagram. The one below shows the decisions an algorithm could make when sorting out a list of objects.

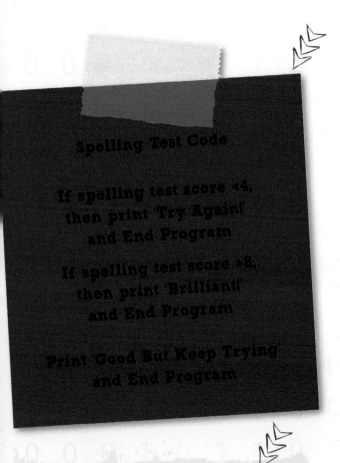

Spelling Test Code

If spelling test score <4, then print 'Try Again!' and End Program

If spelling test score >8, then print 'Brilliant!' and End Program

Print 'Good But Keep Trying' and End Program

Challenge:
Which scores out of 10 would earn the 'Good But Keep Trying' mark in the above code and which would earn a 'Brilliant!'?

Answers on page 31

Is it a toy?

Yes · · · No

Does it have legs? · · · Does it have a handle?

No · · · Yes · · · No · · · Yes

It's a ball · · · It's a teddy · · · It's a cushion · · · It's a mug

Go with the Flow

Programmers need to think through all the possible things that can happen in an algorithm or program and check that all the parts work in the right way and in the right order.

Follow the flow chart

Many coders use a diagram called a **flow chart** to map out their algorithm or program. This helps them to find errors and make improvements.

A flow chart can contain four different shapes or symbols, including an oval, rectangle, diamond and **parallelogram**. These are connected by arrows to show the different stages and flow of information in a program. Each shape or symbol means a different thing.

Flow Chart Symbols

Terminator

Oval shapes show the start or end of a whole program or just part of a program.

Process

Rectangular shapes show that something happens, such as numbers being added together.

Decision

Diamond shapes show where a program makes a decision. This is usually a simple decision such as 'yes' or 'no' or 'true' or 'false'.

Input/Output

Parallelogram shapes either mean that the program accepts an **input** like the click of a computer mouse or **outputs** data such as displaying a message or picture on screen.

STRETCH YOURSELF

Here is a simple flow chart to show an algorithm for how a player makes a move in a game of Snakes and Ladders.

Fix the Flow Chart
This flow chart shows an algorithm for working out why a lamp isn't working. There are some gaps in the flow chart. Can you work out which pieces of circled text go in each gap?

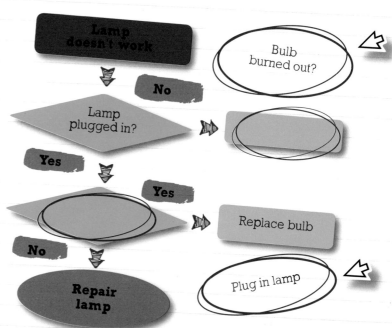

Answers on page 31

COMPUTER Hero!

Frank Bunker Gilbreth was an engineer who enjoyed making jobs as simple as possible. In 1921, Frank introduced the first flow charts to map out workers' jobs. Flow charts would later become popular with computer programmers.

Going Loopy

Loop
Turn round
Shout: "I'm feeling dizzy"
Loop

The instructions in a loop will happen again and again as long as the loop continues

Computers are brilliant at performing the same task over and over again without making any mistakes. Lots of computer programs take advantage of this to get jobs done.

Loops and variables

The repeating parts of a program are called **loops**. These often use little stores of data called **variables**. A variable's value can alter and be used to count things in a program.

Computers use variables in a program to remember things such as a player's score in a game. A variable is given a name and is a sort of box that can hold information such as a number or a series of letters. This is known as a **string**. So, a variable to store your age might be age=9 and another could be name='James'. Variables can be changed by code in the program.

Count on us

Loops are useful for counting events or things, especially when they are used with variables that keep track of how many times something has happened.

The loop below counts down the seconds until a rocket lifts off. Each time the program goes through the loop, the value of the variable Seconds goes down by one. The loop ends on lift-off – this is when the variable Seconds equals zero.

Countdown!

Seconds = 60
Repeat
    Seconds = Seconds -1
    Show on screen: Seconds
Until Seconds = 0

In a loop

Some loops continue for as long as the program runs. These are called infinity loops. Other loops, like the countdown loop on page 24, are told to repeat a set number of times.

Conditional loops are another type of loop. They keep repeating the steps in the loop until something else happens. For example, this algorithm for a shop checkout scanner only allows 10 items or fewer to be scanned. If more are attempted, then the scanning loop ends.

Ten Items Or Fewer

N = 0

N is a variable. It equals the number of items scanned. It is set to zero to start with because nothing has been scanned.

Loop
Scan item
For each item scanned, let N = N+1

One is added to the number of items scanned.

If N > 10, ring bell and display 'No more than 10 items!' and Leave Loop
Loop Again

STRETCH YOURSELF

Fix the Time

Here is a loop that is part of a digital clock program. It's not working properly because it shows the time 02:07 as 01:67. Can you work out which of the three numbered lines below should replace the circled line to get the program working properly?

Minutes = 0 — Minutes is the name of a variable.

Hours = 0 — Hours is also a variable.

Loop

Minutes = Minutes +1

If Minutes = 60, Then Hours = Hours+1

If Hours = 24, Then Hours = 0

 1. If Minutes = 60, Then end loop

 2. If Minutes = 60, Then Minutes = 0 and Hours = Hours+1

 3. If Minutes = 67, Then Minutes = Hours

Answers on page 31

`01:67`

`02:07`

A Bug's Life

Only some programs work the very first time. Programmers expect errors to happen. These errors are known as bugs. Getting rid of bugs in a program is called debugging.

Check and test

Some programming errors are just typing mistakes such as keying in the wrong number or misspelling a command. These are often spotted by carefully checking all the program code. Other errors, though, are more complicated and may take a long time to solve.

Programmers often break their program down into small parts and then run and test each part to try and find the problem.

Testing times

Testing takes place throughout the time a computer program is being developed. Sometimes, computer users are asked to test out the programs. They act as **beta testers** and report back any bugs or problems that they find.

ERROR

Launch failure

Some bugs in programs can be devastating. A bug in the guidance computer of an Ariane 5 space rocket made the rocket veer off target and finally self-destruct just a minute after lift-off in 1996.

TRUE STORY

Moth Bugs In 1947, a dead moth caused a switch to malfunction inside the Harvard Mark II — one of the first computers. The programmers stuck the moth into the computer's logbook. It was computing's first 'bug'!

STRETCH YOURSELF

Catch the Bug

This flow chart shows the parts of a program for playing 'Tag' or 'It'. But one of the arrows is in the wrong place for the program to work properly.

Can you work out which arrow is wrong, and where it should go?

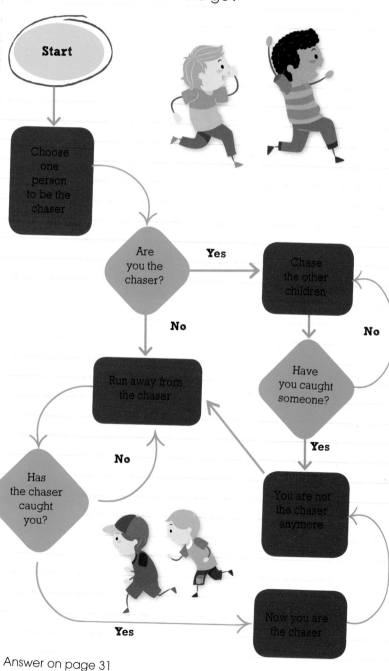

Start

Choose one person to be the chaser

Are you the chaser?

Yes → Chase the other children

No

Run away from the chaser

Have you caught someone?

No

Has the chaser caught you?

No

Yes

You are not the chaser anymore

Yes

Now you are the chaser

Answer on page 31

Coding Careers

Think you might become a whizz at computer coding when you get older? If so, then there may be some great jobs for you when you grow up.

⬇ Working together

In the past, computer programs and code were often written by only one person. Today, many major applications and games need dozens or even hundreds of people to build them.

Some people work out what the program should do, while others write and test the code. Many other coders work on existing programs, writing code for new features or **debugging** problems with the latest program.

COMPUTER Hero!

Jack Dorsey was fascinated by coding as a child. In 2006, Dorsey and his business partner, Biz Stone, wrote the first version of the Twitter social networking app in just two weeks. Over 500 million 'tweets' are now sent every day.

Jack Dorsey

Think big

The programs you use on a computer are often huge projects. A typical iPhone app may have 30,000 lines of code, while a complex computer game can have over a million! Even bigger is the Windows 7 operating system, which contains about 40 million lines of code. Phew!

Young coders – just like you!

Computer coding can be a job for life. For example, Markus 'Notch' Persson was a programming whizz-kid. He wrote his first computer game using BASIC when he was only eight years old! When he grew up, Markus wrote games for Jalbum. He left his job to create his own hit game – Minecraft.

TRUE STORY

World Wide Fun The game Tetris was created in 1984 by a computer engineer called Alexey Pajitnova. Tetris has since been reprogrammed to work on lots of computers, phones and tablets.

STRETCH YOURSELF

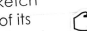

Write a Computer Program

Can you think of a computer program that would make your life easier?

Try to sketch out all of its different parts.

Then, ask yourself these questions:

☞ How would the program operate?

☞ What would the program need to know?

☞ What controls would users need to use it?

☞ What problems can you see in advance?

Glossary

algorithm A set of steps that are followed in order to solve a problem or perform a task.

beta tester A person who tests a computer program that is almost finished to try and find any bugs or problems.

binary Also known as base 2, binary is a number system that contains just two digits: 1 and 0.

browser A type of computer program used by people to view websites on the World Wide Web.

coding Writing the lines of code in a program that make a computer or other device work.

code selection When a program is told to run a particular piece of code after making a decision, such as running the code that says 'Game Over' and giving a final score when the program decides the game has ended.

compiler A computer program that converts instructions written in a programming language into code that a computer can understand and act on.

database A program that allows people to store huge amounts of information on computers with ease.

debugging To identify and remove errors in a computer program.

decimal Also known as base 10, decimal is the number system that you use every day. It contains the digits, 0, 1, 2, 3, 4, 5, 6, 7, 8 and 9.

decomposing Breaking down a complicated task into smaller parts or steps, making it easier to understand and write code.

flow chart A type of diagram that maps out the actions and decisions that occur within a program or part of a program.

input Data or commands that a user enters into a computer using a keyboard or by pressing a touchscreen on a tablet.

loop A part of a computer program that repeats the same steps and instructions over and over again. Many loops are conditional – they continue until a condition is met or an order instructs them to stop.

output The results of a computer's processing and work. Output is often displayed on a screen.

parallelogram A shape with opposite sides that are parallel and also equal in length.

programmer A person who writes computer code and programs, either for fun or as a job.

smartphone Powerful mobile phone that contains a mini computer which allows users to view videos, listen to music and run lots of different programs.

string A type of variable (see below) that stores one or more letters or other characters.

subroutine A section of a program which performs a task and can be jumped back to as many times as the whole program needs.

variable A location for storing information in a program which can be changed by other parts of the program.

Further Resources

Books

How Things Work: Electrical Gadgets
by Ade Deane-Pratt (Wayland, 2013)

Quick Expert's Guide: Computing and Programming
by Shahneila Saeed (Wayland, 2015)

Quick Expert's Guide: Creating an App
by Chris Martin (Wayland, 2014)

Technology Timelines: Digital Technology
by Tom Jackson (Franklin Watts, 2015)

Websites

https://www.commonsensemedia.org/lists/coding-apps-and-websites
A great page containing links to lots of different computer activities and languages to help you learn about coding.

https://www.helpkidscode.com/
A website for parents, teachers and older children.

http://learn.code.org/hoc/1
A video tutorial which helps you use the Blockly coding language to create a simple program.

http://www.light-bot.com/hocflash.html
Have fun programming an on-screen robot called Lightbot.

http://www.scratch.mit.edu
Learn more about coding by creating programs starring Scratch the Cat and other fun characters.

http://www.wordfreegames.com/game/binary-game.html
A groovy game to help teach you how to use binary numbers.

Answers

page 8
Change Decimal to Binary:
16 = 10000
17 = 10001
21 = 10101

page 9
Become a Binary Spy!:
6 = Your middle and fourth finger
10 = Your index and fourth finger
13 = Your index, middle and little finger
20 = Your thumb and middle finger

page 12
Control the Turtle:
* The LOGO program would draw the equilateral triangle (answer d)

* The first and fifth lines should both say 'Forward 100 steps'.

page 13
Robot Rocket Launch Challenge:
Here are the rest of the commands the robot will need in order to reach his rocket.

9. Move forward 1 space
10. Turn to the right
11. Move forward 1 space
12. Turn to the right
13. Move forward 2 spaces
14. Turn to the right
15. Move forward 4 spaces
16. Turn to the left
17. Move forward 1 space

page 18
Can You Fix the Instructions?:
1. Put in bath plug
3. Fill bath with water
8. Get undressed
4. Get into the bath
5. Wash
7. Get out of the bath
6. Take out bath plug
2. Get dressed

page 21
Spelling Test Code Challenge:
* The scores 4, 5, 6, 7 and 8 would earn a 'Good But Keep Trying' mark.

* The scores 9 and 10 would earn a 'Brilliant!' mark.

page 23
Fix the Flow Chart:
* 'Plug in lamp' should go in the blue rectangular shape.

* 'Bulb burned out?' should go in the green diamond shape.

page 25
Fix the Time:
Line number 2 should replace the circled line.

page 27
Catch the Bug:
The arrow at the bottom right of the chart is in the wrong place. To debug the program, this arrow should point from 'Now you are the chaser' to 'Chase the other children'.

Get AHEAD in COMPUTING

TITLES IN THE SERIES

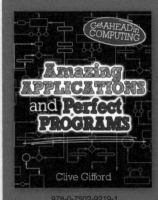

Program Explosion
Operating Systems
Popular Operating Systems
Interface to Face
Data and Circuits
Files in Style
Getting Organised
It's the Business
Text Success
Words and Picture
Sounds and Music
Games, Games, Games
App Attack!

978-0-7502-9219-1

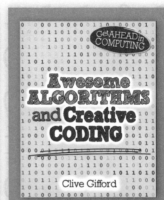

Coding your World
Algorithms in Action
Ones and Zeros
Mind your Language
Languages for Learning
Scratch!
Accurate Algorithms
Get in Step
Decisions, Decisions
Go with the Flow
Going Loopy
A Bug's Life
Coding Careers

978-0-7502-9216-0

A World of Computers
The Incredible
 Shrinking Computer
Here's the Hardware
Let's Look Inside
Data and Circuits
Memory Matters
Imput Devices
More Input Devices
Sounds Amazing
Picture Perfect
Computer Gaming
Mega and Mini Machines

978-0-7502-9213-9

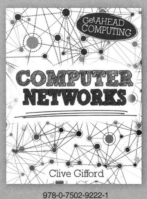

Networks All Around Us
Let's Connect
The Internet
World Wide Web
Web Wonders
A World of Websites
Search Engines
Search and Filter
You've Got Mail
Social Networks
Danger Danger!
Keep It To Yourself

978-0-7502-9222-1

WAYLAND
www.waylandbooks.co.uk